CALIFORNIA

THE GOLDEN STATE

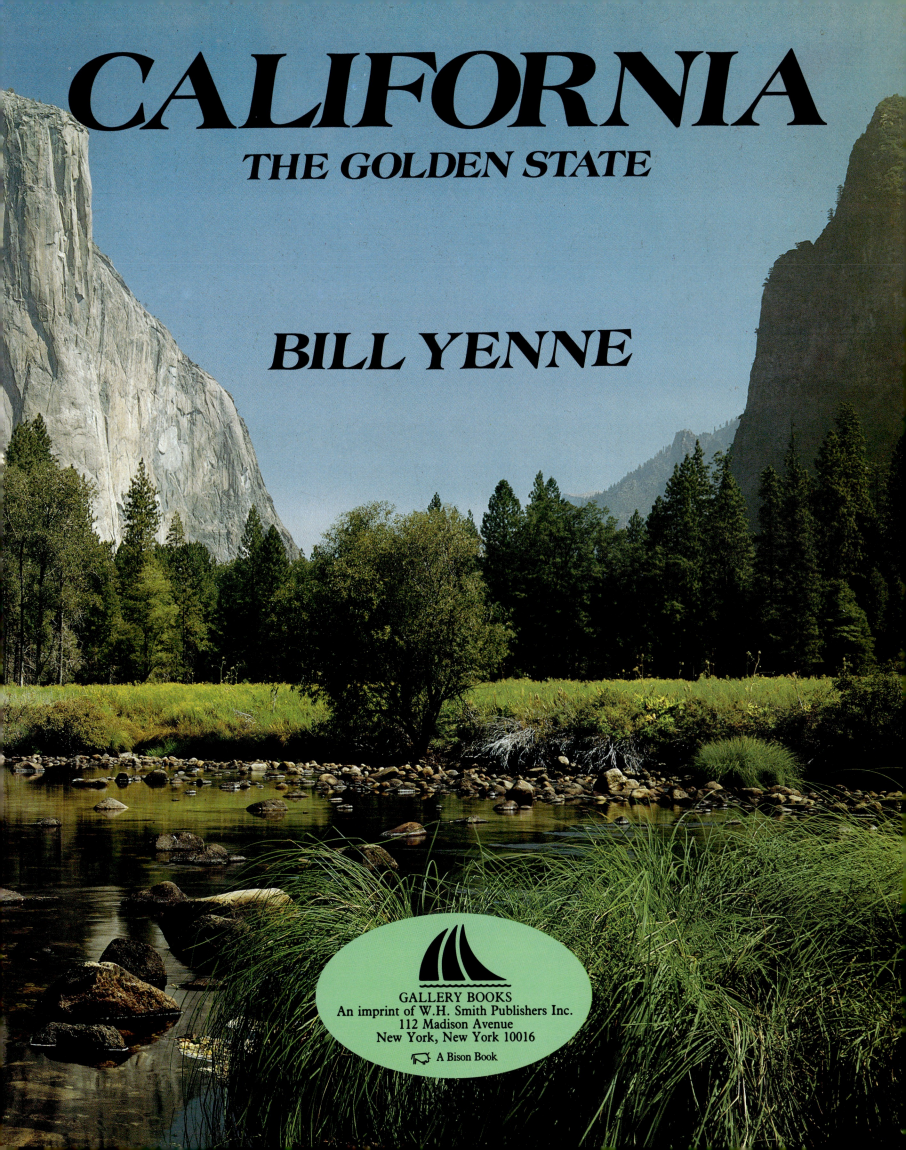

CALIFORNIA
THE GOLDEN STATE

BILL YENNE

GALLERY BOOKS
An imprint of W.H. Smith Publishers Inc.
112 Madison Avenue
New York, New York 10016

A Bison Book

Published by Gallery Books
A division of W H Smith Publishers Inc.
112 Madison Avenue
New York, New York 10016
USA

Produced by
Bison Books Corp.
17 Sherwood Place,
Greenwich, CT. 06830
USA.

ISBN 0-8317-1154-X

Printed in Hong Kong

1 2 3 4 5 6 7 8 9 10

Page 1: The sunset brings a splash of color to pillow-like clouds over Joshua
Tree National Monument.
Page 2-3: The Merced River, in its midsummer low-water stage gurgles gently
through a sun-washed Yosemite Valley.
Below: Large sand dunes and coastal grasses like these at Pismo Beach State
Park in San Luis Obispo County are a common feature along California's
beaches.

Picture Credits

The author would like to thank Jerry Sieve, Douglas Storer and the Freelance
Photographers Guild (FPG) for supplying photographs used in this book.

Tom Algire, FPG 28-29; **Dave Bartruff,** FPG 80 (top); **Marcello Bertinelli,**
62-63, 76 (top); **James Blank,** FPG 10, 17 (top left), 21, 30-31, 52-53, 72, 77 (top), 81
(bottom right), 86 (top right), 87; **Jon Brenneis,** FPG 64; **Buttarazzi,** FPG 22; **Tom
Carroll,** FPG 83 (top); **Ed Cooper,** FPG 42, 44, 60, 61; **Howard Critchell,** FPG
81 (top); **P Dallas,** FPG 82-83; **L Foster,** FPG 19 (top); **Gerald French,** FPG
18-19, 24-25, 49; **E Gebhardt,** FPG 7, 89; **L Grant,** FPG 73; **Farrell Grehan,** FPG
28 (top); **P Gridley,** FPG 84-85, 86 (bottom); © **Hammond Incorporated,**
Maplewood, NJ 6; **Joel Hornstein,** FPG 23 (bottom right); **Kathleen Jaeger** 23
(bottom left), 28 (bottom); **J M Kordell,** FPG 80 (bottom); **Richard Laird,** FPG 68;
Michael Legge, FPG 90 (top); **Constance McCoy,** FPG 12-13; **Messerschmidt,**
FPG 70-71, 71 (bottom); **Miller Services,** FPG 75; **Robert P Morrison,** FPG 83
(bottom); **Suzanne Murphy,** FPG 78-79; **J Randkleu,** FPG 14-15, 37; **Robert
Reiff,** FPG 69; **R Rowan,** FPG 20 (top); **Galen Rowell,** FPG 26, 38 (top); **Otto
Schatz,** FPG 38 (bottom); **C Schwartz,** FPG 2-3; **J Scowen,** FPG 86 (top left);
Jerry Sieve 1, 4-5, 88, 90 (bottom), 91, 92-93 (both), 94-95, 96; © **Douglas Storer,** 27,
31 (top), 36 (bottom right), 38-39, 41 (bottom right), 45, 47 (bottom left), 50, 51 (top),
58 (top), 65, 67 (top); **P Wallick,** FPG 66-67; **L Willinger,** FPG 74; **William R
Wilson,** FPG 58-59; **G Yechiam,** FPG 23 (top); © **Bill Yenne** 8-9, 11, 16, 17 (top
right and bottom), 19 (bottom), 20 (bottom, both), 31 (bottom), 32 (all 3), 33, 34 (both),
34-35, 36 (top and bottom left), 40, 41 (top and bottom left), 43, 46, 47 (top and bottom
right), 49 (all 3), 51 (bottom both), 54-55 (all 4), 56 (all 3), 57, 58 (bottom), 67 (bottom),
71 (top), 76 (bottom), 77 (bottom), 81 (bottom left).

Designed by Bill Yenne

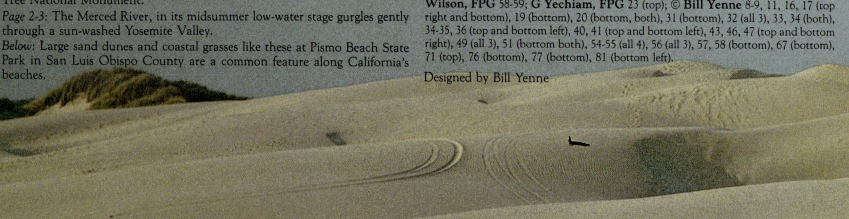

Contents

San Francisco
and Vicinity

California

SCALE
0 10 20   40   60   80 MI.
0 10 20 40   60 80 KM.
State Capitals .... ⊛
County Seats .... ⊙
Canals
Major Limited Access Hwys.
Scale 1:4,400,000

Sacramento
and Vicinity

Los Angeles
and Vicinity

© Copyright HAMMOND INCORPORATED, Maplewood, N.J.

Introduction

California Counties

Welcome to the Golden State bids a sign near the Nevada state line.

It is the land they call the Golden State, a legendary place at the end of the rainbow and at the edge of the continent where the golden sun dissolves into the warm waters of the blue Pacific. California has captured the imaginations of many generations who have come west to share the treasures of its mines and farmlands, walk its sun-washed beaches or stand in the coolness of its redwood groves.

Before the Gold Rush of 1849 when it became known literally as a golden state, California was home to a mixture of diverse Indian tribes. Because food supplies were relatively abundant, little in the way of open warfare took place and the lifestyle was easygoing and peaceful. The major tribes in northern California, the Pomos, Yuroks, Hupas and Miwoks, subsisted on acorns, berries and wild game, while the Chumash of southern California thrived on ocean fish. When the white man arrived, the unconcerned California Indians offered little resistance and easily fell into the pace of life at the early Spanish missions.

The first European known to have arrived in California was Spanish explorer Juan Rodriguez Cabrillo in the early sixteenth century. Sir Francis Drake landed just north of San Francisco in 1579 and claimed what he called 'New Albion' for Queen Elizabeth I, but it was the Spanish who established the first settlements in the Golden State. A mission was founded at San Diego in 1769 and another in Monterey a year later. Father Junipero Serra established a string of missions along a wagon trail called the El Camino Real (The Royal Road), including the mission at San Francisco that opened its doors in 1776, the year that the English colonies on the East Coast issued the Declaration of Independence.

California continued as a colony of Spain until 1822, when Mexico became independent, whereupon California became a semiautonomous colony of Mexico. Gradually more and more Americans came west and the mood predictably drifted toward the idea of an independent California. On 4 July 1846, then-Major John C Frémont led the 'Bear Flag' revolt, proclaiming California's independence from Mexico with the support of the United States. Two years later, gold was discovered at Sutter's Mill in the Sierra foothills and Americans came west in droves. In September 1850, California entered the Union as the 31st state and the first state in the Far West. Another 40 years would elapse before California was contiguous with the greater part of the United States, though it would be linked to the nation by the transcontinental railroad in 1869.

California experienced a tremendous spurt of growth in the wake of the Gold Rush, a growth that turned San Francisco from a dusty mission town into a world-class metropolis practically overnight. After the Gold Rush, the state grew at a modest but steady pace until World War II and the years following, when there was another burst of growth. In 1964 California overtook

7

New York as the most populous of the 50 states. In 1940 five out of every 100 Americans were Californians and by 1980 it was eleven out of 100. Of these Californians, 15 percent are Hispanic, of Mexican origin; 13 percent are Irish; 7 percent are black and 5 percent are Asian.

California's nearly 25 million people live in an area one and a half times the size of New England and have an area second only to Texas in the continental United States. The distance from Smith River in Del Norte County to Winterhaven in Imperial County is greater than the distance from New York City to Savannah, Georgia. California's two largest counties, San Bernardino and Inyo, could swallow Switzerland and the Netherlands with room to spare. California leads the United States in per capita income. If California were a country, its gross national product would rank as the world's sixth largest.

This marvelous state is also a land of contrasts. Within California the tallest mountain in the continental United States, 14,495-foot Mt Whitney, can be seen from the lowest point in the western hemisphere, 282 feet below sea level in Death Valley. The state's environmental diversity ranges from sandy beaches to snow-capped mountain peaks, from freeway-ensnarled urban areas to remote deserts and hill country serviced only by rarely traveled dirt roads. California contains the second and fourth largest metropolitan areas in the United States, Los Angeles and San Francisco. Ninety percent of the state's land area is non-urban, however, and while San Francisco County has a population density of nearly 8000 per square mile, such counties as Alpine and Inyo have but two persons per square mile.

Meanwhile, there are contrasts between the state's urban areas. San Francisco, the state's smallest county, is tiny in land area but it has the greatest concentration of skyscrapers west of Chicago, whereas sprawling Los Angeles is a world of shopping centers and parking lots. San Franciscans pride themselves on an elaborate transit system that includes everything from modern subways to century-old cable cars, while Los Angelenos are lost without their cars.

The California State Park System includes 180 parks and beaches scattered the length of the state and encompassing 723,000 acres. There are more major national parks in California than in any other state except Alaska, and they add another 2,089,398 acres to California's recreational areas.

The state bird, the California valley quail (adopted in 1931), is a familiar sight throughout the state, but the state animal, the grizzly bear (adopted in 1953), cannot be found within the state. Nevertheless, the bear is emblazoned on the state flag and is the mascot of the two largest institutions of the state's university system, the University of California at Berkeley (Golden Bears) and the University of California at Los Angeles, UCLA (the Bruins).

When the Conference Board of Associated Research Councils rated institutions of higher learning in 1983, three California schools were among the top five universities nationwide. The University of California at Berkeley came out on top (with 30 departments in the top ten) while Stanford University (a private institution in Palo Alto) was second with 24. UCLA was fifth behind Harvard and Yale. All of this adds to both the quality of life and to the universal appeal of California.

Join us now for a leisurely tour through a panorama of colorful vistas from America's Golden State.

The Coastline

Mendocino County to the Mexican border and ranks as one of the world's most beautiful drives. It is, however, less a highway than it is a road. It is a four-lane thoroughfare as it passes through Los Angeles, Santa Barbara and San Francisco, but, for the most part, it is a twisting two-lane blacktop hugging the cliffs and canyons of the coastline. The drive from Los Angeles to San Francisco on a valley freeway takes less than a day, but the same trip on Highway 1 can take several days.

Nine percent of California's population lives in these nine coastal counties that constitute 14 percent of the state's land area. In turn, about half of these people live in Santa Barbara and Ventura counties, adjacent to the Southern California metropolis of Los Angeles. Eureka, the county seat of Humboldt County is the largest coastal city north of San Francisco, with 24,000 people. While the north coast is a rugged mix of redwood groves and fishing towns, the coastal cities south of San Francisco such as Santa Cruz, Monterey and Santa Barbara offer a blend of both original and revived Spanish architecture and a pleasant temperate climate.

C alifornia's coast stretches from the 42nd parallel in the north nearly to the 32nd parallel in the south, covering the greatest straight-line distance within state boundaries of any of the contiguous 48 states. Coastal California is a rugged country comprised of breathtakingly beautiful cliffs and long stretches of sandy beach. North of Los Angeles the coastline is surprisingly remote from the state's major centers of population. Of the major cities of the San Francisco Bay Area, only San Francisco itself has an ocean beach. The main street of the coastline is California's Highway 1. It stretches from the redwoods of

The Pacific meets the Golden State. Blue waters pound the rocky cliffs of Point Lobos State Reserve *(left)*, while below a photographer prepares to catch the last rays of the setting sun from a beach near Santa Cruz

A world of contrasts on the California coast. Breathtaking vistas from cliffs on the Big Sur coast *(below)*, and the quiet majesty of a redwood grove in Redwood National Park on the Del Norte coast *(overleaf)*.

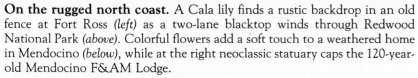

On the rugged north coast. A Cala lily finds a rustic backdrop in an old fence at Fort Ross *(left)* as a two-lane blacktop winds through Redwood National Park *(above)*. Colorful flowers add a soft touch to a weathered home in Mendocino *(below)*, while at the right neoclassic statuary caps the 120-year-old Mendocino F&AM Lodge.

Mankind makes his mark on the coast. The Pigeon Point Lighthouse (*left*) is a prominent landmark on State Highway 1 between Santa Cruz and San Francisco. An oyster farm and a youth hostel on its grounds make it a welcome stopping-off point for travelers from many walks of life.

Fort Ross (*top*), near the mouth of Northern California's Russian River, was established as an outpost by Russian fur traders in 1812. Long since abandoned by its original owners, it has been carefully restored by California State Parks Department archeologists like David L Felton.

Olema (*above*), near Tomales Bay and the Point Reyes National Seashore, is typical of the small quiet towns that dot the state's north coast.

On Monterey Bay. The sardine canneries of Monterey's Cannery Row *(top)* that inspired John Steinbeck's novel of the same name have fallen silent, but commercial and sport-fishing activity still bustles at the city's nearby Fisherman's Wharf *(left)*.

Construction of a sand castle is a major undertaking for this group of castle builders on the beach near Capitola *(above)*.

The Seventeen-Mile Drive between Carmel and Monterey via Pebble Beach is the Golden State's only toll road. The toll is moderate but the views *(right)* are priceless. Each year thousands of visitors flock to Pebble Beach for the 'Crosby Clambake,' a golf tournament once hosted by Bing Crosby.

South toward Santa Barbara. Youngsters investigate the wonders of teeming coastal tide pools *(left)*, while boat owners congregate in the harbor at Santa Barbara *(far left)*.

William Randolph Hearst's enormous castle at San Simeon *(top)*, now part of California's State Park System, attracts hundreds of visitors every week.

Mission Santa Barbara, behind the prickly pear cactus garden *(above)*, was founded by the early Spanish colonists as part of a whole archipelago of outposts along the coast of what is now California, and gave its name to the present-day city.

White sandy beaches and gnarled cypress help make Carmel one of the most photographed scenes on California's coastline.

The Mountains

Two major mountain ranges, the Cascades and the Sierra Nevada, form the backbone of the Golden State. The Cascade range extends south from the Pacific Northwest roughly to the 40th parallel in Plumas County. The highest peaks in the California Cascades, Mt Shasta (14,162) and Mt Lassen (10,466), are both dormant volcanos and are both snow-capped year round. In the Sierra Nevada range there are several peaks between the 39th and 36th parallels that exceed 11,000 feet above sea level, including Mt Whitney, the tallest mountain in the United States outside Alaska.

The counties that make up California's mountain country constitute nearly a third of the state's land area but only three percent of its population. Shasta and Placer counties are home to over a third of the region's population, partly because Placer County is within commuting distance of metropolitan Sacramento. The largest city in the region is Redding, the Shasta county seat.

The mountain counties played an important role in the history of California, because it was in such counties as Amador, Placer, El Dorado, Calaveras and Tuolumne that gold was struck, unleashing an enormous wave of immigration that gave the state its first great spurt of growth. They call it the Gold Country or the Mother Lode, the latter after the huge gold deposit that was theorized to exist but never discovered. Today a few gold prospectors still work the headwaters of the Mokelumne, Stanislaus and American rivers. A few of them make a living, but if anyone has struck it rich recently up in the Gold Country, he's keeping it to himself.

While some dream of the riches that may still lurk under the surface of the mountain counties, thousands flock there every winter for the snow. The ski slopes of Shasta and the Sierra, particularly those near Lake Tahoe, offer some of the nation's best in the way of winter sports. Notable among the resorts is Squaw Valley, north of Lake Tahoe, that hosted the 1960 Winter Olympics.

High in the Sierra. Snow-capped Mt Humphreys (*left*), standing 13,986 feet above sea level, is one of California's tallest mountains. Emerald Bay (*below*) is one of the most beautiful spots along the shores of Lake Tahoe.

Northern California's snow-capped volcanos are a reminder of turbulent times in the Golden State's geologic past. Mt Lassen, seen here from the air in late winter *(top)* and in midsummer reflected in Manzanita Lake *(right),* is the centerpiece of the Lassen Volcanic National Park.

Mt Shasta *(above),* the highest mountain in Northern California, is a popular skiing area.

California's scenic wilderness. South Lake near Bishop *(left)* was created by a glacier, long gone, but not forgotten as one dips into its frigid waters on a hot summer day.

A pair of backpackers *(top)* enjoy a hike through the El Dorado National Forest back country, while the South Fork of the American River *(above)* gurgles down from Lake Tahoe toward the sea.

Independence Day in the small towns of the Sierra. An antique automobile in front of the flag-draped St George Hotel in Volcano (*left*) is a foil for the modified road bikes in front of Volcano's general store (*right*).

This baby carriage decked in red, white and blue bunting (*top*) was photographed by the author on a Mokelumne Hill porch on the nation's bicentennial in 1976. The town's volunteer fire department is always a part of Mokelumne Hill's annual Independence Day parade (*above*).

Reminders of an earlier era. The Gulf Station in Sheep Ranch *(top)* sold gasoline for 18 cents a gallon in the days before unleaded. For the price of real estate, one should inquire inside.

Sonora's White House *(above)* displays an ore car once used in a motherlode mine, while a barn on State Highway 108 *(right)* advertises the wares of the lumber company in Twain Harte, a town named for Mark Twain and Bret Harte, who both once lived in the area.

Passing through. The Kennedy Mine *(top)* is no longer in operation, but it once brought miners by the hundreds to the town of Jackson. Prospectors *(left)* still pan the streams of the Sierra for the yellow metal of which dreams are made.

Mountaineers *(above)* pause along the trail in the Desolation Wilderness, while a narrow road *(right)* winds through hills of the eastern Sierra, cloaked in the golden raiment of autumn.

The majesty of Yosemite. The granite face of Half Dome Mountain *(right and top)* is the dominant landmark in Yosemite Valley and a veritable magnet for mountain climbers from all over the world.

The Ahwahnee *(above)*, Yosemite Valley's grand hotel, offers comfortable rooms with spectacular views.

Wintertime in the High Sierra. Boats huddle at the northern shore of Lake Tahoe (*top*) as snow dusts the peaks that surround the lake. Every winter many visitors (*above*) from California's cities drive to the Sierra to ski and enjoy the snow in places like Alpine Village (*left*).

An early morning frost (*far left*) turns an ordinary thistle to beautiful and delicate crystal.

Wintertime in Yosemite Valley. As the sunshine washes into the stillness of the valley *(above)*, a light breath of mist rises off the icy Merced River.

Yosemite Falls, the nation's tallest waterfall, grows into an immense, roaring vertical river as it is fed by melting snow higher in the mountains *(right)*.

The San Francisco Bay Area

The nine counties upon whose land mass lap the waters of San Francisco Bay constitute only five percent of the state's land area but a quarter of her population. The metropolitan Bay Area ranks between Chicago and Philadelphia as the nation's fourth largest, and its center is San Francisco, the largest city and the commercial and financial hub of Northern California. The City and County of San Francisco are one and the same, the only such city and county in the state. San Francisco is the state's smallest county, with only 91 square miles, nearly half of them the water surface of San Francisco Bay.

San Francisco is the oldest major city on the continent's West Coast and as such is proud and even a bit snobbish about its level of sophistication. It is a pride that many visitors over the years have found to be justified. San Francisco is frequently compared to New York for the quality of its restaurants and performing arts. In per capita terms, it rivals or exceeds all the world's major cities in the number of eateries, and the quality and diversity of its restaurants continue to amaze even long-time residents. The City is home to a world-class opera and symphony as well as several major museums. It is also home to more foreign consulates than any other city in the United States except the nation's capital and New York City, with its United Nations missions. While compared favorably to municipalities many times its size, the scale of San Francisco is more like that of Kyoto or Florence. Unlike many of the world's major cities, it is immensely livable, a city where intricate Victorian houses cling to picturesque hills and where young urban professionals raise their families on quiet tree-lined streets.

For all its cosmopolitan complexity, San Francisco is also a city of business. Its financial district is the headquarters of the world's largest commercial bank (Bank of America) and one of the world's three largest oil companies (Chevron), along with a multitude of other corporate giants including Transamerica, whose distinctive 853-foot pyramid added a unique profile to the City's skyline in 1972.

The other major cities of the San Francisco Bay Area are Oakland, the seat of Alameda county, and San Jose, the seat of Santa Clara county. In the heart of Santa Clara County and reaching north toward San Francisco is Silicon Valley, the center of the nation's fast-growing computer and microprocessor

A world of rich contrasts. The vineyard country of the Napa Valley (*left*) is a short drive from bustling, cosmopolitan San Francisco (*above*). The Noe Valley neighborhood (*foreground*), with its wooded yards and Victorian homes, is in contrast to the skyscrapers of the financial district in the distance. Notable on the skyline are the green copper dome of City Hall at the left and the City's two tallest buildings, the Transamerica pyramid and the dark marble Bank of America Building.

industry, unofficially named for the tiny silicon chips that are produced there. Stretching along the Bay's western shore, the highways and byways of Silicon Valley are home to the sleek modern buildings that quarter the leaders of today's high-technology revolution, and the men and women who will lead tomorrow's high-tech boom.

At the north end of San Francisco Bay, there is another valley whose products could not be more different from those of Silicon Valley, but are equally important to the lifestyle of the Golden State. There is little doubt that the Napa Valley is the premier wine-producing region in the western hemisphere. From this picturesque vale with its delicate climate, wines have gone forth to entice the palates of the world. Even such French vintners as Moet & Chandon have come to the Napa Valley to establish vineyards and wineries on its fertile hillsides.

Victorian San Francisco. Remodeled to its late nineteenth century elegance, an Eastlake-style Victorian home *(left)* greets a new morning. Alamo Square *(above)*, with its neat row of Queen Ann-style Victorians juxtaposed against the skyline, is one of the most photographed views in the City.

At home in the Bay Area. Victorian houses *(top)* are found in all the older towns and cities around the Bay. Built in the late nineteenth century, they survived the notorious 1906 earthquake and today are prized by homebuyers. The town of Sausalito, in Marin County *(below left)*, offers spectacular views of the Bay. Noe Valley *(below right)*, in the heart of San Francisco, takes on the look of a European village under the mantle of the rare snowfall that the City received in February 1976. Telegraph Hill, capped by Coit Tower *(right)*, is one of San Francisco's oldest and most prized residential areas.

The intricate fabric of San Francisco architecture is more than just Victorian homes and the Transamerica pyramid. The Embarcadero Center (*left*) is a complex of office buildings and a hotel that are a model of successful urban design. Many of San Francisco's old piers (*above*) include colorful Spanish-inspired facades. This Sansome Street architects' office (*below left*) is whimsically decorated as an enormous three-dimensional blueprint. The facade of the Ghirardelli Chocolate Factory building (*below right*) is typical of the facades found on many older commercial buildings throughout the area.

The Golden Gate Bridge was completed in 1937, and is listed as the state's leading tourist attraction. Both US Highway 101 and State Highway 1 cross the bridge, which connects San Francisco with Marin County, seen in the distance. The suspension span between the two huge towers was once the world's longest. Painting the bridge in its distinctive rust-preventing International Orange color is a never-ending process. By the time the job is complete at one end, it's time to start over at the other.

Bay Area lifestyles. Sailing (*left*) is a popular year-round activity on the 300 square miles of San Francisco Bay. The town of Half Moon Bay in San Mateo County (*top*) bills itself as the 'Pumpkin Capital of the World' and hosts a pumpkin festival every October that is a delight for area youngsters. The Tathagata Buddhist Monastery in Sonoma County (*above*) is just one of many of the area's diverse religious institutions.

San Francisco's Chinatown and Japan Center help make the City home to the largest Asian population concentration outside Asia. The Peace Tower *(above right)* between Post and Geary Streets at the foot of the Buchanan Street pedestrian mall is the centerpiece of Japan Center, while Grant Street *(above left)* is the main thoroughfare and commercial hub of Chinatown. The multi-tiered building at right is a major Chinatown landmark.

San Francisco by night. The Bay Bridge crosses Yerba Buena Island *(right)* to connect Oakland with San Francisco. The peak of the Transamerica pyramid *(top)* is the crown jewel in San Francisco's nighttime skyline. The famous San Francisco fog *(above)* creeps catlike over Twin Peaks and Mt Sutro.

A drive through the Napa Valley wine country is a feast for the eyes with rolling hills and scenic vistas (*left*), amid which are the wineries like the Charles Krug (*above*) that embody a blend of ancient craftsmanship, timeless technology and modern marketing brilliance. *Overleaf*: The Golden Gate Bridge frames the skyline of the city of San Francisco as sailboats with colorful spinnakers dart about the bay.

The Valleys

Nestled between the coast range and the Sierra Nevada are California's huge central valleys. Named for the two rivers that flow through them, the Sacramento and San Joaquin, these two valleys are agricultural bonanzas. The Sacramento and San Joaquin valleys are one of the world's richest food-producing regions and help make California the top agricultural state in the United States, with a 40 percent lead over Iowa and 44 percent over Texas in cash farm receipts. In the mid-nineteenth century the immigrants came for the gold metal of the Sierra's mines but stayed for the golden sunshine of the great valleys with their rich soil and *two* annual growing seasons.

Today California leads the nation in the production of everything from alfalfa to potted plants. The Golden State accounts for more than 99 percent of the nation's almonds, dates, figs, kiwifruit, olives, pistachios, pomegranates, prunes and walnuts. From California's fields come more than 70 percent of the nation's supply of avocados, broccoli, cauliflower, celery, grapes, lemons, lettuce, nectarines, plums, safflower, strawberries and tomatoes. California leads the nation with a 52 percent share of the fresh-vegetable market, leaving second place Florida with a mere 11 percent share.

Agriculture is a multibillion-dollar industry, and the production of Fresno, Tulare and Kern counties is worth in excess of a billion dollars annually each. In all, the 17 valley counties account for 25 percent of the state's land area and about 14 percent of its population. The two biggest cities are Sacramento, with about 300,000 inhabitants, and Fresno, with about 250,000. Sacramento has been the capital of California since 1854, four years after statehood. Fresno, meanwhile, has grown into the agricultural capital of the San Joaquin Valley as the seat of Fresno County, the state's leading farm county.

Images of California's heartland. San Joaquin ricefields flooded for planting *(left)* amid orchards are right across the road from suburban homes. The state capitol in Sacramento *(below)* bathed in the light of the late-afternoon sun.

The fabric of valley life includes the great California Aqueduct that runs from the Sacramento River deep into Southern California and provides the irrigation that has helped create the miracle of San Joaquin Valley agriculture. The office buildings of Sacramento *(top)* have proliferated with the growing complexity of governing the Golden State. Cropdusters, flying aircraft such as the Grumman Ag-Cat *(above),* help protect the valley's valuable crops from pests.

The Cities of Southern California

Much of the image of California that is propagated in the popular media is generated in the state's Southland. It is an image of palm-lined boulevards, swimming pools and movie stars. Los Angeles grew from a sleepy mission town in the nineteenth century to the largest city in the state well before World War II. The majority of the postwar immigration into the state benefited Southern California, allowing Los Angeles to become the nation's second most populous and San Diego to become the state's second most populous.

The image of Southern California as a land of glamour and excitement is perpetuated by the fact that the nation's motion picture and television industries are based here. The majority of the shows that Americans watch each week on network television originate in Southern California. Every night Americans from Montana to South Carolina and from Utah to New Hampshire watch their favorite imaginary heroes driving the real streets of Los Angeles County. Hollywood became the movie capital of the world in the 1930s and still holds the reputation even though most of the studios are located in other Los Angeles

County cities, such as Burbank, Culver City and Westwood. Southern California is also home to a number of the world's most famous amusement and theme parks like Marineland, Knott's Berry Farm and the most renowned of them all, Disneyland.

Southern California is more than a land of make believe, it is also the center of the nation's aerospace industry and home to the major operations of Lockheed, Rockwell International, General Dynamics, Hughes, McDonnell Douglas and Northrop.

The three counties of metropolitan Southern California—Los Angeles, Orange and San Diego—comprise 6 percent of the state's land area but contain nearly half the state's population.

In 1984 Southern California played host to the 23rd Summer Olympics, with most of the events taking place in the scattered venues of Los Angeles, Orange and adjoining counties. The Olympics, however, was but one aspect of the athletic activities that flourish in the sunny Southland. From the jogging and roller skating in Venice to the surfing at Huntington and Malibu, nonorganized sports have helped to shape and define the Southern California lifestyle.

Symbols of the Southland include the Hollywood Hills with their famous sign and the freeways of the San Fernando Valley, the nation's archetypical suburb. *(below).*

Elements of the LA style range from the Rolls-Royces and Mercedes Benzes of palm-lined Beverly Hills *(left)* to the intimacy of the Hollywood Bowl *(above)*, used for both classical and pop concerts.

Southern Californians gave a rousing welcome to the USA team as they entered the LA Memorial Coliseum for the 1984 Summer Olympics *(top)*. The Los Angeles Olympics was the largest and most profitable Olympics ever held, and it was enjoyed by more spectators than any other.

LA landmarks include the Griffith Park Observatory *(opposite)* and the buildings of downtown Los Angeles *(above)*, viewed from the Harbor Freeway. Directions and locations in Los Angeles are reckoned in terms of the freeways, whose familiar names include the Golden State, the Santa Monica, the Hollywood, the Ventura, the Santa Ana and the San Diego. The Los Angeles freeway system is a modern engineering wonder.

LA sunsets. On the left, the sunset washes the skies over Century City with breathtaking color, while at the right, the street called Sunset—Sunset Boulevard—winds its way out of Hollywood and on to Beverly Hills. Unlike Beverly Hills and West Hollywood, which are independent cities, the original city of Hollywood is actually within the Los Angeles city limits.

The endless summer. Beginning with the affluence that begat the surfing craze and the car craze of the 1960s, Southern California and its beaches became a youth paradise. When the Beach Boys sang 'Let's go surfin', they had a whole nation of young people willing to follow *(above)*. The elements of that lifestyle range from sunbathing to surfing at Malibu *(above right)* and the beach life *(left and right)* amid the oil derricks of the Orange County coast.

For many former beach boys, the lifestyle has been transformed to include ownership of yachts and sailboats, and what better place to anchor one's yacht than at Marina del Rey in the heart of Los Angeles County coastline *(overleaf)*. The three counties of Southern California each have more boat berths than any other county and among them have nearly half the state total. Los Angeles County alone has a total of 17,184.

The magic kingdoms. Southern California's theme parks are a wonderland of fantasy and enjoyment. Cinderella's castle and the nightly fireworks show *(upper left)* are the highlight of a trip to Disneyland, which is connected to the Disneyland Hotel by the monorail *(far left)*. At the left, two young visitors are greeted by a favorite Disney character on Disneyland's Main Street USA.

Marineland of the Pacific in Palos Verdes *(above and below)* treats visitors to live shows featuring such creatures as killer whales, dolphins and porpoises.

With the Pacific in your backyard. The exclusive seaside towns of Laguna Beach *(left)* and Emerald Bay *(top)* contain some of Orange County's most expensive real estate. Avalon Harbor *(above)* is on Santa Catalina Island, 30 miles off the Orange County coast.

The Del Coronado Hotel, overlooking San Diego Harbor, is one of Southern California's finest hostelries.

The sights of San Diego include beaches such as the one at La Jolla *(above)*, the mission San Diego de Alcala *(right)* and California Tower in Balboa Park *(far right)*. Below, the city's modern skyline forms a backdrop for the boats riding at anchor in the harbor.

The Deserts

The great Mojave Desert consumes the majority of four counties and 20 percent of California's land area. Most of the 6 percent of California's population that make their home in Riverside, San Bernardino, Imperial and Inyo counties live in cities near the edge of Los Angeles and Orange counties. Much of the balance of this vast region is a stark yet beautiful land of yucca trees and shimmering mirages. Inyo and San Bernardino are California's largest counties, and the latter is the largest county in the United States. Encompassing an area of 20,164 square miles, it is bigger than nine of the smallest states and larger than Maryland and New Jersey combined. It is the hottest region in the United States and the western hemisphere. A tem-perature of 134 degrees Fahrenheit recorded in Death Valley was the highest registered on this side of the planet and is just two degrees cooler than the hottest temperature ever recorded on earth. The lowest elevations in California, Death Valley and Imperial Valley, are also situated in the desert, and both are well below sea level.

The parched and barren desert possesses a back country that has claimed the lives of many who have penetrated its rugged interior, but its resorts, such as Palm Springs and Rancho Mirage, afford a striking contrast. Palm Springs and the sur-rounding area have come to be the dwelling place of a microcosm of America's rich and famous. Celebrities like Bob Hope, Frank Sinatra and former president Gerald Ford have made their home in the clean dry air of this glittering jewel in the Mojave. Though temperatures frequently soar past the 100-degree mark in the summer months, winters in such places as Palm Springs and Hemet offer a delightful climate to many seasonal residents, who range from the glamorous and powerful to the retired people from the upper great plains and mountain states who come south in campers to beat the snow and frigid weather that grips their homeland.

Life in the desert. The Joshua tree's spiny appearance *(left)* belies the fact that it is a member of the lily family. Scotty's Castle at Death Valley *(below)* is one of the Mojave Desert's most renown oases.

The presence of water in a barren land is evidenced by the lush fairway of a Palm Springs golf course *(above)* and the buckhorn cholla *(below)* that thrives here in the Desert. Rare but heavy rainstorms in the desert cause flash floods, which in turn erode the dry washes such as the one at the right, seen running through the mudstone hills below Zabriskie Point in the heart of Death Valley *(right)*.

Sunset over the desert. Badwater (*left*), a pool of salt-laden water in Death Valley at the foot of the Panamint Mountains, marks the lowest point in the western hemisphere. A seemingly endless wavy line leads across the Mesquite Flat Dunes (*above*) toward the Grapevine Mountains.

The stark beauty of California's deserts. Manly Beacon *(below)* stands like a monument to the geologic forces that created it, while sunrise reveals the delicacy of the desert primrose *(overleaf)* at Kelso Dunes.